# L



# and Billy

**by Pauline Cartwright**
**illustrated by Rob Mancini**

HOUGHTON MIFFLIN HARCOURT
School Publishers



Printed in China

ISBN-10: 0-547-25270-6
ISBN-13: 978-0-547-25270-4

11 12 13 14 0940 18 17 16 15 14 13
4500443494

Lucy wanted a bird for her birthday. The whole family went to the pet shop.

"There must be a hundred birds in a row!" said Thomas, her little brother.

Lucy looked at each bird carefully.

Some of them drooled. Some of them had collars. Some were big. Some were small.

Finally, Lucy found the bird she wanted. It was a parakeet with straight green feathers and a curly yellow beak.

Lucy decided that her bird's name would be Billy.

Lucy told Dad, "Parakeets can learn to talk. I'm going to teach Billy to say his name!"

"You will have to try hard," said Dad. "It takes a bird a long time to learn to talk."

Lucy cleaned Billy's cage. She made sure he had water. She weighed his bird seed.

Every day she would say to her parakeet, "My name is Billy."

Lucy's brother Thomas would also say, "My name is Billy."

"Don't do that!" Lucy said. "I'm teaching Billy to talk."

Soon Billy learned to sit on Lucy's finger. Lucy would pet his floppy head and say to him over and over, "My name is Billy."

“My name is Billy,” Thomas said over and over.

“Don’t do that!” Lucy told him.

Sometimes Lucy let Billy out of his cage.
"My name is Billy," she called as he flew by.
"My name is Billy," called Thomas, too.
"Don't do that!" Lucy told him.

One day, Lucy was busy doing her homework. Thomas stood in the door and said, "Lucy, come quick! Billy just talked."

Both children ran to Billy's cage.

Lucy was so excited she could hardly talk herself!

"Billy, talk to me," she said. Then she waited for Billy to talk.

Billy looked at Lucy with his little black eyes. His beak hardly moved, but Lucy heard him talk.

"Don't do that!" Billy said.
Lucy couldn't believe her ears.

# Responding

## TARGET SKILL Sequence of Events

Lucy wanted a pet that could talk. Copy the chart below. Think about some things that happened first, next, and last in the story. Use the chart to show the steps Lucy took to teach Billy.

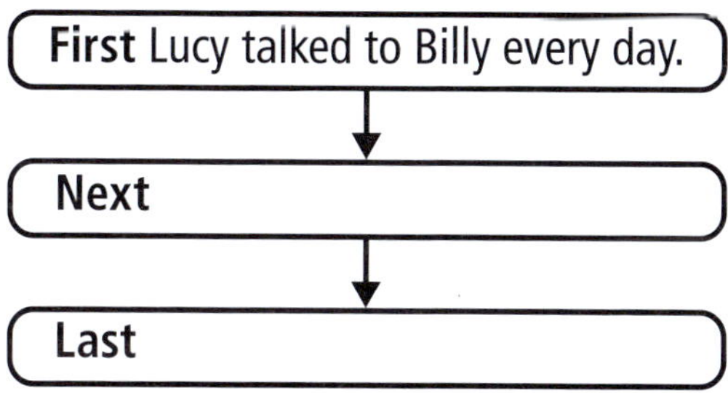


## Write About It

**Text to Text** Think about a book you have read about a pet. Write some sentences that tell what happened in the story. Be sure to use order words such as *first*, *next*, and *last*.

**TARGET VOCABULARY**

| | |
|---|---|
| collars | row |
| curly | stood |
| drooled | straight |
| floppy | weighed |

**TARGET SKILL** **Sequence of Events** Tell the order in which things happen.

**TARGET STRATEGY** **Infer/Predict** Use clues to figure out more about story parts.

**GENRE** **Realistic fiction** is a story that could happen in real life